MORPHEUS POSSESSED

The Conflict Between

Dream and Reality

W. E. GUTMAN

CCB Publishing
British Columbia, Canada

Morpheus Possessed:
The Conflict Between Dream and Reality

Copyright ©2015 by W. E. Gutman
ISBN-13 978-1-77143-241-2
First Edition

Library and Archives Canada Cataloguing in Publication
Gutman, W. E., 1937-, author
Morpheus possessed : the conflict between dream and reality
/ written by W. E. Gutman. -- First edition.
Issued in print and electronic formats.
ISBN 978-1-77143-241-2 (pbk.).--ISBN 978-1-77143-242-9 (pdf)
Additional cataloguing data available from Library and Archives Canada

Cover design by the author.

Cover background: Grey paper texture: © valkot | Canstockphoto.com

This book is printed on acid-free paper.

Disclaimer by author: References to persons, real or fictitious, alive or dead, are contextual and intended to lend thematic legitimacy to a largely objective account of manifest reality.

Extreme care has been taken by the author to ensure that all information presented in this book is accurate and up to date at the time of publishing. The publisher cannot be held responsible for any errors or omissions. Additionally, neither is any liability assumed by the publisher for damages resulting from the use of the information contained herein.

Publisher: CCB Publishing
                  British Columbia, Canada
                  www.ccbpublishing.com

*I don't know whether I was then
a man dreaming I was a butterfly,
or whether I am now
a butterfly dreaming I am a man.*
Zhuang Zhou (369-286 BCE)

Also by W. E. GUTMAN

JOURNEY TO XIBALBA:
The Subversion of Human Rights
in Central America
Reporter's Notebook. Non-fiction. © 2000 (out of print)

NOCTURNES — Tales from the Dreamtime
Fantasy fiction. © 2006

FLIGHT FROM EIN SOF
Fantasy fiction. © 2009

THE INVENTOR
Historical fiction. © 2009

A PALER SHADE OF RED — Memoirs of a Radical
Autobiography. © 2012

ONE NIGHT IN COPAN —
Chronicles of Madness Foretold
Tales of mystery, fantasy and horror. © 2012

ONE LAST DREAM
Screenplay. © 2012

UN DERNIER REVE (One Last Dream)
Screenplay (French-language version).
Translated by the author. © 2012

ALL ABOUT EARTHLINGS:
The Irreverent Musings
of an Extraterrestrial Envoy
Dystopia, parody © 2015

And he dreamed, and behold!
a ladder set up on the ground
and its top reached to heaven;
and behold, angels of God
were ascending and descending upon it.
Genesis, 28:12

OTHERWORLDLY REALMS

Paris, 1949. Four years had passed since the end of another war to end all wars, a mere ten since the City of Light had reveled in the gentle radiance of hedonism and insouciance. Shell-shocked and enfeebled, my hometown was slowly stirring from a post-Occupation gloom that would constrict its soul long after the flesh wounds had healed. Traumatized, dazed, the French were now surrendering to a world of make-believe that hearkened to a time long since gone. They sought comfort in childish evasions what they could not yet accept as the stark reality of inglorious defeat.

I was twelve.

"For homework," said Monsieur Delorme, our 6th-grade teacher, "study chapter five in your history book and be prepared to defend, with examples of his early triumphs, the assertion that, despite his catastrophic losses on Russia's frozen steppes and his humiliating rout at Waterloo, Napoleon was one of our greatest military strategists."

Four years after the end of the Second World War, France was more inclined to wax nostalgic about empire than ruminate over the infamies of its mortifying collaborationist past.

"Also, write a one-page essay; talk about your dreams. We'll discuss them in class tomorrow."

"My dream," wrote one of my classmates "is to become a famous battlefield commander. It makes no sense to wage wars," he argued with puerile bombast, "unless you're determined to win them." Clearly, he was parroting a long-discredited canard. History was not this boy's strong point. He hadn't learned that wars are not won; they're just suspended for a time while new ones are being hatched.

Marianne, a precocious utopian whose Résistant grandfather died fighting the Germans, imagined "a better world, a world without conflict." How could she have known that a world without conflict is a world that has come to an end?

"I dream," wrote the son of a business tycoon who pledged to follow in his father's footsteps, "to be a millionaire." Daddy must have assured him that the family fortune would be his to squander as he saw fit.

There was a wannabe cowboy, a gendarme, a ballerina and a Michelin-star-aspiring chef. Fabien, the class Adonis whose good looks were dwarfed by his colossal ego, sought movie stardom; Gaston — the adulation of doting fans on soccer stadia. Marcel dreamed of boxing rings, championship bouts and big paydays. Three pupils, the ones who chose to sit in the back of the class, turned in blank papers. They had no dreams. Heredity or circumstance, they must have reckoned, had fated them to the quiet dignity of shop keeping, the tedium of public service, or the dreariness of factory work.

There were no budding poets, storytellers, artists or composers in this post-war generation of mine, no stargazers, no would-be philosophers, not a single explorer, seafarer or entomologist, no humanists, no mystics, only uninspired pragmatists and one lone starry-eyed pigtailed romantic who mistook hope for fait accompli.

I grew uneasy. As these infantilisms were being read aloud, I asked myself whether I'd misconstrued the teacher's assignment. Would my essay elicit ridicule? Imagining a better world, less yet praying for one, as cloistered penitents and worshipers of every faith had done for centuries, I knew, does not bring about a better world. Quite the reverse, faith, in a number of infamous cases [the Crusades, the "Holy" Inquisition, the Reformation, sectarian wars, wars of conquest, annexation, colonization and ethnic cleansing] had brutalized, debased and dehumanized the world, not healed it. Millions of people had been impacted by these upheavals, my tribesmen included, as oppression, persecution, torture and death stretched from the Land of Canaan to Babylon, from Judea and Samaria to Egypt and Spain and Portugal, from Germany to Eastern Europe, the Balkans, the Caucasus and beyond. The scriptural fears and hatreds that inspired these abominations continue to fester, kindling archetypal quarrels in faraway places between people of which the world knows nothing.

I had also learned at an early age that no

matter how noble, a goal is a distant objective, not an upshot, that wishes are like beads of quicksilver — too fickle, impossible to seize; that hope is a treacherous chimera, a placebo, an antidote against unmanageable reality. Whereas a dream, ah, a dream, not some reverie or fanciful longing but a *dream,* the sort that snatches you as you sleep, holds you captive and steals your breath away, a dream is a one-of-a-kind, spur-of-the-moment, unrepeatable, ceaselessly mutating, thrilling and at once terrifying eventuality that dies and is reborn in the blink of an eye in another time and place.

In my trademark cursive (in those days good penmanship was an asset) I'd written:

"I dream a lot. My dreams define me. Many of my nocturnal escapades involve flight. I am strolling in the middle of a tree-lined street. Chestnut trees, I think. I spread my arms and take off like a bird. I feel elated, freed from the shackles of a turbulent childhood. Sometimes, instead of a takeoff roll, I jump up, as if propelled by invisible coils, each time bounding higher, feeling ecstatic and proud of a feat that people on the ground, no bigger than ants, find as startling as it is implausible. Soon, I find

myself near the portals of deep space where cries are never heard, tears never seen, and the human drama is all but a distant and nebulous conjecture. I survey my home planet with a mixture of nostalgia, pity and disquiet, suspended as I am at a point beyond time. I fear I can never make a safe descent from such astral heights. So I lean forward, my arms swept back to reduce drag, my fingers arched in a camber of my own design and I become airborne again, an eaglet hitching a ride on an auspicious updraft. I am both winged night stalker and a spectator at my own air show. I keep revisiting the dream as often as I can."

My essay aroused neither fits of laughter nor the scorn I had anticipated. Instead, it was greeted with a long, frozen silence, the stern, vacuous mien of uncomprehending youths and a glint of praise in my teacher's eyes. It was perhaps that look of astonishment and reticent admiration telegraphed by Monsieur Delorme that would spark in me the urge to live by the pen. Or did it kindle the heretofore-dormant genes that my progenitors had bequeathed? After all, wasn't my maternal grandfather a distinguished journalist, poet and jurist? Wasn't his son, my uncle, a noted commentator and art critic? Didn't one of my father's distant cousins, a novelist, win the Nobel Peace Prize?

◆

I enjoy my dreams, even when they daunt me. What I like best is that they let me stray into the same otherworldly realms where lunatics abscond when awake. I become a quick-change artist: I can move from eccentricity to sacrilege, from wantonness to mysticism to full-blown insanity without the condescension, the stigma, the vilification. I can think impure thoughts; indulge in blasphemy, engage in vile, obscene acts, proffer incendiary opinions and exasperate those who wander in my crosshairs. I can surrender my life for a lofty cause. I can even kill if I get the urge without ever wasting a single soul. Sometimes, folly is a refuge from the irrationality of reason, from a world hostile to freaks, mavericks and heretics. A dream is where one's basest whims, most sordid fantasies, bottled-up resentments and grandest cravings can all be gluttonously quenched.

When reality is too much to bear, all that's left are the dreams. I accept them for what they are. I try not to read too much into them, not to speculate about their origins or agonize over the effect they might have on me or—by writing about them—on others. Doing so would distort the dreams and encourage those who might chance upon these wispy, tattered mental images to misinterpret them, to jump to absurd conclusions.

What I strove for in this narrative is spontaneity. Many dreams, too faint to recollect or reenact with any degree of accuracy, were left where they came from—the now inaccessible black abyss of my subconscious mind. Too painful to relive, too personal for public consumption or too damning, many others were ultimately deleted from a hasty and potentially incriminating first draft.

Caveat lector.

I DREAM, THEREFORE I AM

There would be no reason to dream were it not for reality. Whatever form it assumes, reality is immutable. It is useless to talk about it in metaphysical terms. It lacks imagination. It is too straitlaced, neurotic. Like instinct, it is myopic. It can't possibly replicate the fragmented structure and hallucinatory character of the dreams that it [reality] attempts to mimic. On the other hand, dreams, like intuition, are far-sighted yet, like gossamer, too delicate to handle. Once dreamt, they dissolve, only to mutate and breed in a dizzying profusion of forbidden dreams, titillating dreams, sacrilegious dreams, infectious dreams.

It's a dream-jungle out there.

♦

Teeming with nagging premonitions, doubts, false starts, confusion, fears, remorse and unfulfilled longings mangled by the passage of time, my dreams run on two parallel and converging tracks. Casual bystanders will be transported to the dark regions of a restive psyche viewing itself. They will be treated to the spectacle of a conflicted being trying to grab hold of the visions that haunt his nights and make sense of the waking hours that spawn them. Insightful observers will embark on a voyage to the antipodes of reason. The crossing is stormy, buffeted by gales of nostalgia and pounded by lamentations on the inevitability of linear time. My dreams seem to be sending a constant stream of SOSs: I keep running aground on the shoals of an intractable identity crisis. To dream: Perchance to be, to navigate vast unearthly dimensions that no psychoanalyst, popular myth or fraudulent spiritualist can chart.

My dreams also rise up in defiance of physical reality. They telegraph repressed emotions, buried memories, inhibitions and phobias. They betray a lust for inaccessible pinnacles and a fondness for fruitless expectations. They rebel against the banalities that often challenge the thinking man.

Dreams: Winged abstractions that question the validity of conventional canons. Dreams: An array of uncommon ideas and bizarre perspectives. Dreams: Fits of therapeutic disobedience. Dreams: Echoes of the bewildering ugliness, cruelty, cupidity, trickery and injustice dreamers endure when awake and stirring. Dreams: A cure against ossified creeds. Dreams: Cathartic bouts of temporary insanity. Crafted in the deepest recesses of the mind, staged against eerie backdrops, spoken in esoteric tongues, they challenge reality, defy the status quo and strike at doctrinaire beliefs. Dreaming, for an untold number of people, is an escape tunnel from enforced, often unbearable actuality. Dreams respond to frustration, anxiety, pain, anger, despair and hope by offering a few milliseconds of tonic escapism — against hours of conscious but uncontrolled contemplation spent rationalizing the past while vainly attempting to divine the future.

♦

Limitless and everlasting, the world of dreams is a dimension where inhibitions and scruples are left at the door. It's the flip side of a reality vigilantly managed by often dissimilar but tactically congruent interests whose reciprocal aim is to restrain the errant ways of radicals and nonconformists—of dreamers. Awake, man is condemned to be free but arbitrary laws, a shadowy judicial machine that grinds men to a pulp, synthetic social covenants, rigid customs and traditions, the prying eyes and ears of a paranoid political authority and the hypocrisy of the rabble, repeatedly overturn his sentence. Conscious, he lives in a realm where no crime, however odious, can be committed without the consent of the perpetrator and the loud applause of silent accomplices. Conscious, he is under constant scrutiny. Asleep, he is under no obligation to conform. He can surrender to his basest instincts, defy authority, settle scores, and roam unhindered as far as his imagination—or dream-induced psychosis—will take him.

Like art, dreams need not be beautiful, inspiring, politically correct, socially redeeming or even relevant. Their sublime absurdity, surrealism, cunning and wantonness are what infuse them with essence, context, originality.

Dreams lack a definable objective. When the dreamer gets lost, it's because his dreams stray from course like a rudderless vessel. Therein lay their verve, their galling fertility.

Unlike reality, a dream need not have a "meaning." A dream *is* its own meaning. To dream is to *be* in a space and time computed by an errant self.

THE STUFF THAT DREAMS ARE MADE OF

I've had a surfeit of dreams. Most are so wispy and mercurial that I'm not always able to remember them or fit the pieces into a cohesive whole. Some last less than a heart-beat; others linger for a time of their own choosing. Many are unintelligible. Many more, retrofitted somewhere on the fringes of consciousness, assume a new geometry and take on a life of their own. All are idiosyncratic. There is an oddness about them — they are thematic and unnervingly cyclic: I'm headed home or office or a hotel or train station, and I invariably wind up somewhere else after being forced into a series of Escher-like detours and thrust in situations that can only be described as Kafkaesque. Or I'm on an ocean liner, bidding farewell to a person whose identity is never revealed. I fall asleep. The horn warns visitors that the gangplank is about to be uncoupled and the captain invites them to disembark. I wake up ten thousand miles away in some improbable exotic locale. I smell saffron and curry in my mind's nostrils. I hear the tinkle of finger bells. His eyes closed, shrouded in a cloud of bluish haze, Ravi Shankar plucks a wistful sitar. Every human emotion, every subtle feeling in man and nature find expression in the mystic harmonies of an ancient Vedic hymn-inspired raga. Reminiscences of an earlier incarnation, from sinner to sadhu, drift across my field of vision, then vanish. Half naked, his face daubed with ash, his sunken eyes staring into a hallucinogenic void, a holy man exhales a lungful of ganja and places a cadaverous finger on my forehead:

"You shall be reborn from dream to dream. Dreams shall be the path of your transfigurations. They will outlive you." The arcane message resonates within me; it makes perfect sense while the dream unfolds. It becomes unfathomable once the dream evaporates.

◆

Sometimes I enter the dream stark naked. I'm not ashamed of my nudity but I scramble to find something—a rag, an old newspaper— anything to avoid discomfiting people along the way. I remind myself that I'm in puri- tan/promiscuous America, convinced that, had I been in France where I was born, my bare ass would have been greeted as the polit- ical statement it was meant to make. I fanta- size, even as I dream, that I will be presented with the Legion of Honor and kissed on both cheeks by Monsieur le Président de la Répu- blique and, later, awarded a César [the French Oscar] for my courageous performance. Then the dream, like a badly edited film or an in- congruent run-on sentence, jettisons me into yet another undreamed-of locale.

◆

I often dream I have the gift of ubiquity. I can replicate myself and be in several places at once—a useful skill that confounds my tor- mentors, all of whom waste heavy ordnance on the ever-moving target I have become. I can transport myself at will, basking on Grenada's nutmeg-scented silvery beaches, strolling the

Champs Elysées, attending a Broadway show, admiring a Velásquez, a Goya and a Bosch at the Prado in Madrid — simultaneously. Here you see me, here you don't. I did all these things in my wakeful state, and they filled me with joy. But these nighttime capers do not always turn well. I often get hopelessly lost on the way to or from some impromptu destination. The harder I try to reconnoiter my surroundings, the more entangled I become in the mazelike trails of my runaway id.

Dreams, at best, are impenetrable, wayward. They evoke abstract, warped landscapes. They spawn grotesque characters. They hatch aberrant scenarios and force dreamers into awkward, often absurd situations. They stalk and hijack unwary sleepers, lay bare their most secret longings and unmask their obsessions and phobias. For all their quirks, misleading clues, dead-ends and truncated climaxes, dreams are the portals to the soul. I've never been able to cross the threshold.

DREAMSCAPES

Last night, I dreamed that I was trying to open a door. A key was in the lock. It was the right key but it just kept turning and turning. It then began to warp, then it melted, like candle wax. The dream may be emblematic of my longings and struggles and defeats. I have my demons. Some have chased after me since childhood. They quickly matured from the Perrault and Grimm fairy-tale ogres, witches and warlocks, Stoker's vampires and Shelley's jerry-rigged monster, from my dizzying tumbles into bottomless ravines, to the man-made monsters of discord, greed, corruption and war. Other evil spirits materialized over the years. In my dreams I do what these fiends allow me to do to confront them, crush them. But I'm not Hercules. From his genes or by conscious imitation, I seem to have acquired a few of my late father's virtues. Yet heredity is a fickle donor. Its legacy travels in an "as-is" conveyance in which some of my father's own stowaway demons hitched a ride: Depression, horror at man's inhumanity to man—both his parents, two brothers and a sister perished in one of Hitler's slaughterhouses—vexation at the ingratitude of the people he had helped, dismay at the absurdity of life. Born poor, of humble origins, a simple man filled with compassion, an honest country doctor, a healer who shed bitter tears when his first patient died, he could abide neither the fragility of the human body nor the maddening inexactitude of medical science. He kept telling me that everybody is insane, but that only the bravest dare let go. Maybe I'm not as brave as I should be. Maybe it's too soon to let go. Maybe it's my kismet to live to the end in excruciating lucidity, sentient and aware of everything, especially the dreams, the ubiquitous, the inescapable dreams to which I surrender night after night.

◆

Someone is trying to break into our house. As I struggle to resist this intrusion, my wife turns into a pillar of salt. I try to fire my revolver at a featureless assailant but the weapon turns to putty and bullets dribble out of the barrel like globs of boiling semen.

◆

I flex my right biceps. A capillary bursts and my arm turns blood red. The entire right side of my body begins to sag from this massive sub-cutaneous hemorrhage. I ask my wife to call for an ambulance but she's on the phone, talking to her sister on Long Island; she cannot be disturbed. I'm eventually taken to the hospital and the dream dissolves.

The dream transitions from fade-out black to milky gray. I'm in the street on my way home, but I don't remember where I live. No one seems motivated to help.

I then look for my car in a subterranean garage. I meander in tunnels crawling with small, slithering creatures that pop underfoot. I wake up, confused and infinitely more tired than when I went to sleep.

♦

My wife is dressed to kill. She says she wants to go for a walk, alone, on Sixth Avenue. I ask if I can join her but she says no. Using telekinesis (or is it quantum theory) I teleport to Sixth Avenue and look for her. I pass by all the emporia we used to patronize when we lived in New York. But she is nowhere to be found. I then hear a voice:

"Do you fear death," asks Moondog, the "Viking of Sixth Avenue," as we meet on 53rd Street. A small crowd of faceless interlopers gathers to watch us spar.

"No. I fear disease, decrepitude. Most of all, I fear pain."

"Do you believe in God?" Blinded at an early age, Moondog, a confirmed atheist, eggs me on. "Do you, do you?"

"Only insofar as he is unknowable."

"What do you crave most?"

"Knowledge."

"What is knowledge," he sniggers.

"That which can only be learned in minute fragments and over a finite period of time cleverly computed to prevent what is knowable from being revealed all at once."

"Careful now," warns the avant-garde

musician. He leans toward me, his lifeless eyes searching for my presence, his horned helmet hovering menacingly over me. "Knowledge embodies what is *already* known. What is knowable — but as yet unknown — is the province of speculation, not verifiable fact."

As I spin it, I ascribe no importance to this fantastical encounter. The pulsating neon world around us — on this side of the street is the *3 Deuces* jazz club; next door, *Club Carousel*, *Club Samoa* and *The Onyx* are aglow in the slick blackness of night; across the street *Jimmy Ryan's Bar* beckons late night crowds — all adding color to an otherwise *film noir* scored by Charlie Parker and redolent of heroin and hash, syncopated music and luridly made-up ladies of the night.

After some reflection, unimpressed by my oblique construal of God, insisting that God never spoke to him, not even in a dream, Moondog charges at me and exclaims: "God stands for Gigantic Obstinate Delusion." The word, he warns, contains a coded message:

"Dream at your own peril."

◆

Roaming the teeming streets of an unrecognizable metropolis, I panic when I realize I can't remember in what hotel I'm registered. Following a number of dizzying circumambulations on thoroughfares that heave convulsively under me and morph with every step I take, I spot the hotel ... but the room I'd checked in is nowhere to be found. I travel from floor to floor, climbing double spiraling sets of stairs and riding an elevator with inoperable doors. At last, I reach the room. I am greeted by my double.

"Welcome to my dream," he says. I look at this meddlesome avatar and wonder what his embodiment might signify. An inner voice reminds me that having no answer to the questions I ask is far less troubling than being swamped with answers to questions I never pondered.

So much for the esoteric nature of dreams.

◆

I'm running errands in Brooklyn but I can't remember where to get off. A subway employee wearing a suit of armor tries to help but none of the names he mentions sounds familiar. I call my mother [deceased in 1973] on my cell phone and, whimpering, I tell her that I've been diagnosed with Alzheimer's. She says she'll call a friend who "knows the neighborhood." I never get to my destination. Instead, I find myself trying to read a giant comic book but the pages are torn and the images are distorted and blurry. Faceless people around me redirect my attention: My wife is running to catch a train. Sprinting alongside, a man asks her, "Where did you stay in Lisbon?" Meanwhile, trying to ascend a steep, slippery alley, I keep sliding back to the bottom. Sisyphus extends his sympathy and cautions:

"Prudence makes short trips seem longer."

♦

The Public Defender's Office has hired me to plead the fate of a faceless woman. I lose the case. The woman is bitter. I ask her to give me her hand. She does. I take it into mine and explain that I'd done everything I could on her behalf. I take a deep breath and I find myself floating hundreds of feet above a large body of water, maybe a huge swimming pool or a lake. The woman is standing on a Bailey bridge. She waves at me. I hover motionless in the air then I dive, head first, in slow motion, into the pool below. I sink to the bottom and resurface unscathed. I wake up panting, aware that I'd held my breath.

In the next sequence, I'm aboard a hospital ship on which I'm supposed to undergo treatment for an undisclosed ailment but I'm being ignored. No one tends to me. As soon as the ship docks in some fictitious port of call, I sneak out, climb over the railing and scramble onto the pier. As the vessel slips out of its moorings and glides away, I realize that I'm barefoot and that all my belongings are still on board. Before me are three open roads. One of them stretches steeply uphill. I trudge on and the dream fizzles out.

◆

They're after me but they wish me no harm, I keep telling myself without conviction. Lurking in a corner of a split-screen dream, bearing stiletto smiles, two junkyard dogs warn me against undue credulity. Symbolism within symbolism, I note. No matter. All I feel at the moment is impatience and annoyance at the veiled hints, at the same enigmatic insinuations that elude me as I take flight on these nightly evasions. So I dream on to see what other clues might come my way.

♦

It begins somewhere at the edge of a gray, nameless town, a cookie-cutter replica of a thousand gray tank towns, on a gray street senselessly named after some tree or flower — Elm or Poinsettia, Hibiscus or Pine — deep inside a gray house I cannot physically enter but which, as circumstances dictate, allows me transcendental ingress. Don't ask me to explain. I rarely try to decipher my dreams; I depict them as they evolve. Just accept the notion that I can sometimes watch myself from afar.

Glancing through the window, I see a gathering. Spectators? I can't tell. Anyway, they're all dead and they're *attending* the life of a dreamer as if it were a morality play. The dream is filled with so many abstractions. I can't find the words.

"Abstractions," I hear myself asking, smelling subversion, "what does that mean?"

"Things felt but not readily verbalized," I answer with calculated vagueness. The dead look at me with paper-pusher eyes that betray ignorance and stupidity.

"Don't fret, they're dead," a disembodied voice assures me.

Well, not exactly. Let's say these bureaucrats are trapped in a long and irreversible coma of intolerance and mulishness. They're numb and lifeless—if you overlook the hostility in their eyes. The man they have come to observe runs through the mist in slow motion. I can't see his face. The dream fades out momentarily, as if obscured by a passing cloud. I find myself moving through a blinding fog. The dream resumes and pans toward the man. I recognize him. He is *me!* Holding a lantern close to his face, my clone tells the dead they will never be resuscitated. Their diehard values will keep them entombed in a bog of ignorance and triviality. The dead snicker. They don't care. Their brand of mortality keeps them warm and secure. And the dream melts away.

◆

I occupy a sumptuous high-rise on Manhattan's upper West Side. I go out in the morning on some errand. When I return, I can't find my apartment. Every door I unlock opens on an unfamiliar setting—a coffee shop, an office, a library, a beauty parlor, a funeral home. The anger this fruitless quest ignites jolts me awake.

◆

Some nights are so dark, my sleep so deep, that they spawn no dreams, no false starts, no detours, no missed trains, no frantic attempts to get back to who knows what or where. Take that early morning at the Valley Colonoscopy and Endoscopy Center when the gastroenterologist probed, simultaneously I believe, my colon and my esophagus, and I discovered once conscious and stirring that this was not where I'd intended to go before surrendering to the Propofol. It was just an imitation of death, minus the wake, the flowers, the mourners and the post-interment libations.

◆

On one of my frequent nocturnal escapades to Paris (I never stopped yearning for the city of my birth), I meet Jean-Paul Sartre at *Les Deux Magots*, the trendy rendezvous café where he, his mistress, Simone de Beauvoir, Pablo Picasso, Ernest Hemingway, Albert Camus, James Joyce and Bertolt Brecht have gathered. We're sipping a vintage Monbazillac in slender, fluted glasses and gazing absently at a stream of passers-by.

Sartre is an old friend but, frankly, I've become more interested in *being* than *nothingness*, even on a metaphorical level. All my adult life, I'd waded through the marshlands of philosophy, prowled the minefields of Kabbalah and Zen, more to exercise my brain than to seek a particular existential path. I'd struggled with Maimonides, Kant, Spinoza, Nietzsche, Schopenhauer and Marx. A brief, wary fling with "deity" did more to confuse than enlighten me. God had granted me some of his spirit but he never revealed his logic. The mental pirouettes the concept entails had exhausted me and—was it age, cynicism or creeping indifference—I'd become a nihilist whose most enduring preoccupation was to ease into and survive an ill-fitting world not of my own making. By then, I had rejected all doctrines and schools of thought, and broken most social contracts. I was slowly turning into a recluse. My writings, quirky, irreverent and satirical in the beginning, had turned into improvised explosive devices designed to inflict dismay. I discovered in me a need to stun people with unsettling truths and disquieting ideas long before I learned from George Orwell that "freedom is the right to tell people what they don't want to hear." All I knew is that individuals — not society, laws, religion or rituals — give meaning to life, that one can live it as passionately and honestly and creatively in the middle of the desert as one might in the din and bedlam of a big city.

"If you insist on pleasing others at your own expense," Sartre whispers in my ear, "let them add their own punctuation to the ideas you advance and see how quickly they disfigure everything you stand for."

"Sorry, Jean-Paul; I'm going to have to put you back on the shelf."

♦

I work in a small, dark, dilapidated office crammed with tiny, rickety desks. I have no idea what my job entails. Everybody blames everybody else for the waste, the general incompetence of the staff and the abysmal indifference of the overseers. The windows are fake — painted on it seems — the doors have no handles, just large bent nails. I prick my finger and small, blue globules seep out of my swollen finger. When I look closely, I notice they are tiny blue fish.

◆

I'm invited to dinner. Halfway through a very skimpy meal, I discover that I'm wearing pajamas. For reasons that the dream fails to clarify, I take the pants off. Fearing that I might be suffering from an early onset of dementia, I start to run. The ground under me is soggy and muddy. My hosts yell out:

"When can we have you for dinner again?"

I yell back, "Right away. You hardly gave me anything to eat."

Then they ask, "Would you care for a toothpick?"

To pick what, you cheapskates, I murmur to myself.

◆

I find myself on yet another ship. There are no other passengers; the crew is gone. A magnetic mine is attached to the hull. I manage to uncouple it and I toss it into deeper waters. I then steer the ship out of my bedroom and into the living room where my (late) parents are watching television.

"Playing sailor again," they ask in unison.

We all play at being something. Fathers and mothers play the parenting game. Wives and husbands act out roles for which they are mutually unsuited. Children play at being sons and daughters. Teachers play educators. Moses played lawgiver; Jesus played anointed "redeemer;" Pontius Pilate played governor of Judea while Tiberius played Roman emperor. Crusaders and inquisitors staged massacres and their victims, mere extras in a cast of thousands, acted as martyrs. Prophets and mystics and popes played at being in a world apart from the human sphere. Kings and queens play at being monarchs; their sub-jects—at being vassals. Hitler played Hitler and Mussolini played Mussolini. Stalin and Mao and Pol Pot and Ceausescu and Saddam impersonated Caligula. Joseph McCarthy, a drunkard and a liar consumed with hatred, played senator. Historians toy with the past; psychics trifle with the future. Soldiers play war; cops and robbers play cops and robbers. Politicians masquerade as common men and sell themselves to the highest bidder; they just don't call it prostitution. Bankers play Mo-nopoly with other people's money; they just don't call it usury. Clerics play the soul-saving game and their congregants play at seeking salvation from a deaf, dumb and blind supernatural entity that plays hide and seek from the pinnacles of his non-existence. *Papa* played doctor and *Maman* played homemaker. People at their funerals played mourners. The mourners went home, ate, slept, defecated and copulated and played at life until they too died and grievers attended their services. I played at being a newsman and a writer and a paladin until my dreams reminded me that this too was nothing but a senseless performance. One day I will play dead.

It's all one big, hilarious, heartbreaking, sordid, ghastly charade.

♦

I am appointed "Director of Special Projects" at *OMNI* Magazine [where I worked more than 20 years ago]. I have an elegant office and the job involves nothing *special*. I am unhappy with my attire so I rush home to change. As I enter my apartment, I note that everything is submerged under water. I find a vintage seersucker suit and gray suede shoes and put them on. I rush back to my office.

I worked at the late-great New York City-based futurist publication, *OMNI*, until it died of advertising malnutrition and corporate neglect in 1995. For years, I kept dreaming that I was back at my desk, performing fictional tasks in a fantasy setting that did not seem to change from dream to dream. I knew that my old colleagues—Patrice Adcroft, Steve Fox, Frank Devino, John Evans, Pamela Weintraub, Ellen Datlow and Phil Scott—long since resettled elsewhere, were ghosts revived for the occasion, but they were my ghosts, tactful, discreet, self-effacing, like mourners at a wake. I felt comfortable in their wraithlike company. They imparted substance to unreality.

As in previous dreams, this most recent installment found me at my desk, leafing through imaginary manuscripts, consulting with the late Kathy Keeton, talking on the phone with Isaac Asimov and Ray Bradbury, Arthur C. Clarke and Harlan Ellison, Robert Silverberg, Frederik Pohl, Robert Heinlein and Carl Sagan, brainstorming with artists and photographers, planning "special projects" that would never see the light of day. Now aloof and reticent, my colleagues were slowly fading in the background then dissolving like wisps of smoke in the wind. I called them one by one but all I heard was one long collective lament. Then, someone from the personnel office handed me a check, the last one she said remorsefully. I was being "terminated." I blacked out. As the dream resumed, I found myself lying in a coffin-shaped recliner. Then, one by one, my old colleagues reemerged, walked up to me and placed stacks of cash on my chest. "To help you get back on your feet," they chanted. I was moved, immensely grateful. I woke up and I knew that I would never return, except perhaps in my dreams, to that office on Broadway and 63rd Street where, for a short time, I got paid to dream in the company of other dreamers.

◆

I'm on a train headed from New York to Miami. The conductor looks at my ticket and informs me that I have to change trains in Timbuktu. I review the twists and turns that have marked my life and I concur:

"Timbuktu? Why not? That makes sense. That makes perfect sense."

◆

Two young men, ostensibly brothers, are paying me a visit. Both engage in annoying behavior—changing the settings on my satellite radio, playing violent video games on the TV and making a mess in the kitchen. In the next scene, they are both in my bed. The sheets and blankets are covered with spaghetti and splattered with sauce. I'm so incensed that I threaten to shoot them.

◆

I'm attending a wedding reception (spouses unknown) or is it a birthday party? I've been assigned a narrow table at the back of the hall. It's noisy; children are running amok and screaming, causing me great displeasure. Why the hell am I here, I ask myself. I hate parties and I'm not especially fond of children.

◆

I'm in a rooming house looking for a studio. There is none left, the manager explains apologetically but she offers me a bed in a dorm where the only occupant is an old woman who introduces herself as a lesbian.

I introduce myself as a dreamer. "Thank heaven!" she exclaims, "a fellow mutant."

◆

My wife proudly shows me her new iPhone and points to its latest feature:

"It self-destructs," she says.

"That's great," I reply. "They should all self-destruct." I don't like cell phones and I detest people who use them in public. I fantasize that a super-deadly electronic virus has disabled all cell phones. I wake up waxing nostalgic about an era when humans communicated with smoke signals.

◆

A distant voice says there's a party on the second floor of an unnamed hotel. I run up the stairs. I open one door; the room is empty. Another room hosts a lecture. A funeral service is in progress in the third. The fourth is teeming with cows no bigger than mice. I hear myself gagging on a scream that dies on my lips.

◆

Finally, my script, *One Last Dream*, is made into a movie. I attend the premiere in Mumbai. The setting, characters, dialogue, direction and camera work bear no resemblance with what I'd originally conceived. My wife tries to comfort me: "It's not that bad." I'm disgusted and heartbroken. I am reminded of Sartre's comment about letting others insert their own punctuation.

At the post-premiere party I chat with Barbara Bush. She tells me she is so nauseated by the neocons that her political convictions have shifted "well to the left."

◆

Somewhere in the middle of a convoluted dream during which, as usual, I search for something, I find myself on a narrow, dark alley teeming with ghouls. I manage to escape this segment of the dream. I am naked. I make desperate efforts to reach an elusive destination. I get lost at every turn.

◆

I sit at the piano and play a concerto of my own composition. The piece is redolent of Rachmaninoff, Saint-Saens and Tchaikovsky. Played in the upper ranges of the keyboard, the notes tinkle like diamonds cascading into a crystal bowl. I'm amazed at my virtuosity. Toscanini is at the podium. There's no audience. I keep playing an incidental opus I know

I shall never be able to recreate when I awaken.

◆

On another visit to Paris, I'm headed on foot to my favorite hotel on Avenue du Maine. As Tour Montparnasse recedes behind me, I realize that I can't recall the name of a roadhouse I've patronized dozens of times before. I can't even remember on what side of the street it's located. Soon I no longer recognize the city I know so well. Devastated, I wake up weeping.

◆

I'm in Grenada. I misplaced the green, red and yellow canvas bag in which I keep my passport, travel documents, watch and house keys. I ask the hotel manager to help me find it. He hands me a pulley and points to a zip line.

"Take it all the way to the end and, while aloft, ask people on the ground if they've seen your bag."

Green, red and yellow are the colors of the Grenadian flag. One corner of the flag is adorned with ripe nutmeg. It reminds me of a ripe vulva.

The island dozes in mindless serenity, an

overgrown chunk of coral sprouting from the scintillating turquoise sea like an oasis in a desert's unbroken desolation. It's low tide. The surf tugs gently at the flotsam of sea moss and broken shells scattered on the slick sandy shore. Purple clouds glide past a waxen moon, baring an amber and cobalt sky. Pressing low against the sea, the remnants of a distant storm fade away as one last streak of lightning splashes the eastern horizon with a silvery glow.

Sharma's young body glistens through the water. Her chocolate skin feels like wet porcelain and her buttocks, firm and spirited, rest against my groin as her long, willowy legs encircle my waist. Hardened by lust, her purple nipples poke about my chest. I take her that way, far from shore, my feet firmly anchored in the soft silt-like sand lining the shallow lagoon. Facing the sea, feeling her warmth coursing through my veins, I look past her searching eyes until the last wave of pleasure tells me it's time to thank Sharma and exit the dream.

♦

Then there's Reena. I can't see her clearly in

the dark but the black satin form writhing in my arms reaffirms her heady reality. Clouds disperse, letting moonlight in through the open shutters. Her eyes glisten like black pearls but she winces and her ivory smile turns to grimace. It's hard to tell if it's pleasure or pain. She swears it's okay through the eighth month, and I know she's lying, but I go in deeper yet, plowing her life-bearing young body, overlooking the gamy odors, thinking of someone else until the images fade away one by one as I feel myself coming.

◆

I'm meeting a few friends at the long-defunct Los Angeles landmark restaurant, the Brown Derby. Being obsessively punctual, I arrive early and wait. Optimists are always late, pessimists always early, and cynics always on time, I quip. I'm barefooted and not wearing underwear. Conscious of my nudity in a realm that frowns upon it, I crawl on my heels toward a house. I ring the bell and the occupant opens the door. I beg him to lend me a pair of boxer shorts. Taking pity, he hands me one. The dream takes me back to the restaurant's lavatory. I'm still unshod and I'm wading in urine. I have to make. I sit on the toilet and try to shut the door but the door swings in two directions: If I push it one way I expose myself to the restaurant patrons; if push it in the other direction people in adjacent stalls can see me. "If it's not one thing, it's another," I remark blandly. Predictably, the friends who were supposed to join me for lunch never show up. Fuming, I remove all my clothes, walk out and stroll in the buff on the sunny side of Wilshire Boulevard.

♦

I'm on a flight to Honduras. Nervously twiddling their rosaries, praying with a fervor born of faith or fright, passengers around me cross themselves again and again as they recite the *Pater Noster* and call on every holy mortal in the pantheon of sainthood. Holding on for dear life to traveling companions, they survey the fast-rising ground with unmasked trepidation. Fearing death can be deadlier than dying. Landing at Tegucigalpa's Toncontin Airport, they know, requires both great piloting skill and a willful surrender to fate. Wedged between the garbage-strewn slopes of a narrow and densely populated ravine, the runway tilts perilously downgrade. If banking into final approach is a white-knuckle affair, even for the most seasoned pilots, diving at full-throttle with the wings teetering some twenty feet from the brink is nothing short of gut-wrenching. This is no tame three-point landing. Main carriage and nose wheels strike the sloping runway with unexpected force. Reverse thrust jolts the aircraft, triggering powerful vibrations. Overhead luggage bins fly open. Several oxygen masks tumble out of stowage. Wrathful, touchdown in this teeming, grimy, poverty-stricken Central America capital, I reflect, will set the tone, pace and mood for a dream-long descent into hell.

In a series of staccato-like changes of scenery, I find myself on the tarmac, then on a foul-smelling Diesel-burning bus, then in town, seated at a table in a small coffee shop behind St. Michael's Cathedral. I ask the waitress for directions to my hotel (a hotel I know well and have patronized in the past). She points hesitantly at a fork in the road and tells me to bear right. I know from experience that, in these parts, people will lie or lead you astray rather than admit to not knowing. Benevolent deception is one way to save face. I find myself roaming a city with which I'm intimately familiar. And, predictably, I get lost.

♦

A sudden gust of autumn wind sends shivers through the branches of an old weeping willow. A few leaves fall earthward. As they reach the ground, as if pulled together by some magnetic force, the leaves merge and fuse into a full-screen dream in which a sudden gust of autumn wind sends shivers through the branches of an old weeping willow. As they reach the ground….

♦

It's a gloomy, squally night in the North Atlantic. The ship is heaving and pitching and rolling. Thirty-foot waves lift the stern in the air and the propellers grind and moan as they spin idly out of the water. The stern slams back against the churning sea and the prow rises then sinks violently, as if swallowed by a giant trough, beneath the water line. Passengers seem unconcerned as I levitate briefly off the deck. Then in the distance, I see lights glittering in the dark. It's Madeira. We dock in Funchal. An old friend who grows onions for a living tosses several bulbs from the wharf onto the deck. He then climbs aboard. We embrace. I don't speak Portuguese so I address him in Spanish. We talk about the worsening world situation. He disembarks. I return to my cabin. I munch on a raw onion as if it were an apple and the ship heads back into the eye of the storm.

◆

I'm a guest at the Tanya hotel but I can't remember what room I've booked.[1]

"Where's your key," asks he concierge.

"Beats me."

"Go to the reception desk. Someone there will assist you."

"Where is it?"

"Take the elevator at the end of the hall and go to the ninth floor."

I step into the elevator and press "9." But the elevator zooms to the six hundred and thirteenth floor. I look at the panel and discover that there is no ninth-floor button. I get off

---

[1] *The Tanya is an 18th century Kabbalistic work of Jewish spirituality, psychology and mysticism. It summarizes millennia of Jewish wisdom to answer the great personal and existential questions of life. It is said that only one out of four finds in it a path to serene righteousness. The others either lose their faith, die, or go insane.*

and call for the "down" elevator. I get on, thinking that it will take me to the ninth floor. That floor doesn't exist and I wind up spending the rest of an exasperating dream riding an elevator that only travels sideways and never stops.

An old Jewish mystic addresses me through the elevator speakers:

"Your exertions are easily explained: You're an intellectual," he says with noticeable sarcasm, "an 'intermediate,' an 'in-between,' a human who suffers because you have not yet managed to totally transform the evil within you to good; a vestige of it still remains."

♦

I need to cross railroad tracks but a train stands in the way, motionless. I board the train. It suddenly lurches forward, picks up steam and thunders along at full speed toward an unknown destination. I ask the conductor to let me off but he says I have to wait until the train stops at the next station. I get off and find myself in an unfamiliar setting. Bewildered, scared, I'm on the verge of tears. Faceless people ask me where I'm headed.

"I don't know."

"Where do you come from?"
"I have no idea."
"Who are you?"
"An intermediate."

♦

My wife and I are in Monterey, my favorite city in the Golden State. The city is playing host to the French Navy. I meet sailors and chat with them in French. I stopped smoking thirty years ago but I puff on a *Gauloise* for the occasion. The captain invites us to a party later that evening but we can't attend because we live in New York, the dream is too short and we'd miss our flight home.

♦

Following a brief interview, I'm hired to do an unspecified job. I don't know who my employer is. I ask what my responsibilities are but all I get are blank stares. I spend the rest of the dream trying to figure out what this is all about.

♦

Two women ring at our door and offer to cook

"magic" mushrooms.

"What do you need?"

"A frying pan and palm oil," the women reply in unison.

I demur. "Palm oil is high in saturated fats. It's bad for your health. Besides, trees are grown in plantations in Third World countries where criminally lax environmental regulations encourage illegal logging, lead to deforestation, impact endangered species and contribute to climate change."

"We don't care. That's what we use. The pan, please."

I look for a pan. The one I find is filled with tears. I use it to douse a huge forest fire. The fire spreads, uncontrolled, across my field of view. The women curse me. But the animals of the forest rejoice.

◆

I'm having lunch at my favorite midtown Manhattan greasy spoon. Sitting at the next table is a man who looks like a pug.

◆

I'm out for a stroll on Amsterdam Avenue. The weather is balmy, the sun is shining and, looking south, the skyscrapers gleam like silver daggers against an azure expanse. Yet people are all bundled up, shivering, their shoulders arched, their heads pushing against an icy squall. What the hell is going on, I ask myself. Then I remember that I live in California, not New York, and that I must exit the dream. This insight fills me with sadness. I awaken from a dream too abstruse to decipher.

"What drives men," a disembodied voice utters as I stir, "is the reassertion of ego." Some dreams, I reflect, escape interpretation by resorting to non-sequiturs.

♦

I'm headed north on California's Highway 14 toward the southern edge of the Sierra Nevada. It suddenly dawns on me that the car I'm driving isn't mine so I press on and reach a parking lot at Red Rock Canyon. The attendant directs me to an area where he says my car is parked. Hard as I try, I can't find it. Instead, I wind up in an immense, labyrinthine hotel where every corridor is a dead end. A little girl asks me to help her look for her father but we keep running into blood-splattered walls.

◆

I bid farewell to my apartment. Everything is
in disarray. I discover mementos of my childhood—Maxie, the stuffed monkey I cuddled
with in my crib; the baby blanket whose hem I
fondled between thumb and forefinger as I fell
asleep; the toy fire truck my father had bought
on one of his travels; a Tintin adventures al-
bum; a matchbox lined with cotton in which
I'd kept an iridescent beetle. Overcome with
nostalgia, I'm reminded I have to go to work. I
grab a briefcase. It's not mine. I arrive at my
office. I don't know where I am. My eyebrows
fall like dead leaves in autumn.

◆

At the newspaper where I work, someone has
printed what must surely be a prank headline:
"Dreamers finish last." I react with curiosity,
not anger or alarm. Then I find myself on a
crowded public conveyance. A man is smoking and ashes from his cigarette fly into my
eyes. I protest. The man unsheathes a knife.
My arm telescopes some twenty yards and I
yank a branch off a tree. I am about to strike

him but I wake up before any blood is shed.

♦

There's a commotion. I step outside. I hear the whir of helicopters in the background but I don't see any. The next thing I remember is that a nurse is examining me. She tells me I'd fainted and was out cold for about half an hour. Did I faint or nod off from exhaustion, I ask. The nurse laughs. She unbuttons her blouse and offers me a rosy teat heavy with milk. "*L'chayim*," she says. "To life."

It figures. I'm lactose intolerant.

♦

At first, the creature (I have no other word to describe it) materializes out of thin air, a bird-like feline — a griffin — sporting rows of mean-looking fangs and talons. The creature slowly morphs into a less menacing, more kitty-like animal. It slinks toward me then, purring, it nestles in my arms. Its expression is one of love and serenity but people warn me not to trust it. I respond that it's not in my nature to reject affection. The creature smiles then pounces on me and buries its fangs in my neck.

♦

My wife and I are seated on the sofa, staring at a wall.

"Be patient," I say, "*The Honeymooners* will soon be on."

Holding a floppy-eared puppy in one arm, his other arm extended in front of him, a sleepwalking Ed Norton emerges through the wall, moseys toward the kitchen and inspects the contents of our refrigerator.

♦

I'm headed home from a weekend in the country spent with acquaintances. The journey is long and I fall asleep at the wheel. When I wake up, driving though a town I do not recognize, I realize that I'm penniless, hungry and old. I must have left my wallet and other belongings with the people I visited but I don't remember their names, address or anything else about them. I roam the streets in a panic, aware of my vulnerability in a strange place that doesn't seem to acknowledge my existence. I enter what looks like an inn, looking for a handout from some charitable patron. No one responds. Desperate, I execute the Masonic sign of distress several times in a row. Rising from the back of the restaurant, three tall men in full Masonic regalia walk toward me. One of them rips my shirt off and jabs the business end of a large wooden compass at my naked left breast and barks:

"How do we know you're not an undocumented alien flashing the sign of distress so you can sneak into this country?"

I look at the apostate brother with incredulity and sadness. Am I being blackballed?

"My name is Hiram and I'm the Widow's Son," I plead.

"Then die."

♦

The phone rings. It's my doctor. He wants to see me. I arrive at his office in the blink of an eye. Every consultation cubicle has been turned into a sickroom, with bunk beds filled with writhing, moaning patients. I ask one of the staff what the doctor wants and I'm handed a sheet of paper. It's blank.

♦

It's night in dreamland and I'm crossing an open field. A large hole in the ground attracts my attention. I get closer and place my hand in the hole. I retrieve three rag dolls, each swaddled like a mummy. Their faces express pain or disgust. I can't say for sure. One by one, I undo their wrappings and they vanish.

◆

I'm in a hotel room in an unidentified locale. The bed is littered with hundreds of pills, every one a different color. I don't remember if I took any and I can't decide which one to take. There's a knock at the door. Someone says, "Let me in." I refuse to open the door. A finger, then five, then the whole hand snakes in through the keyhole. I bite the fingers repeatedly, savagely, to no avail. The dream shifts. I'm in a taxi with a fellow journalist. When we part, I ask him to keep in touch.

"I'm not looking for a binding correspondence," I say. "Just write when you can."

He looks at me and retorts, "Sorry. I'm going home to Antwerpen. You're an 'in-between,' a rabble-rouser. I don't want to get involved."

◆

I'm headed home from the pool and I scramble to catch the subway. The train is jam-packed. I strain to read the overhead transit network map. I know I have to get off somewhere and transfer to another line, but which? I know I'm not in Paris, London or New York. I panic and get off at the next station. As I stand on the platform, bewildered and frightened, I realize that I don't remember where I live. I try to gather my thoughts but I draw a blank. I weep and explain my predicament to a subway employee. He tells me not to worry:

"These things are common at your age."

I protest, assuring him that I know who I am, where I was born, what I do for a living. "I just can't recall where I live."

The employee pledges to get me home, "safe and sound."

I slowly stir awake but I still can't remember where home is. As the cobwebs scatter and vanish, it dawns on me that I live in California. I am numb and exhausted. I ask myself: "Is this how full-blown dementia begins?"

♦

I accept, reluctantly, an invitation to attend an unspecified function at an undisclosed location. Much to my chagrin, I must wear a suit. I choose a black velvet ensemble, a pink shirt and a black silk tie. As I unfold the shirt and am about to put it on, I notice a gaping hole in the back.

"Never mind," I say to myself, "I'm wearing a vest; no one will know." I wake up, relieved to have been be spared the boredom of small talk with people the dream had the decency not to incarnate. I make a mental note to decline future invitations.

♦

I'm skiing down a steep, slick street and I can't stop. When I reach the bottom, I barely miss being run over by a truck. I remark that in an autobiography a writer reinvents himself whereas in fiction he discovers who he really is.

♦

I'm riding an elevator on my way up to my Manhattan apartment but I can't remember on what floor I live. I press a button at random. I don't want to betray my utter state of confusion to the other riders. I get off. The hallway is dark. I feel my way around and quickly discover that I'm on the wrong floor. I go back down to the lobby where the postman is sorting the mail. I ask him if he knows where I live. He says:

"Sure, it's quite simple. Take the square root of the hypotenuse, multiply it by the gross national product and divide it by your Social Security number. You live in apartment 4-F."

◆

Thousands of people and I are stranded at a railway station waiting for a train that never comes. Railroad officials say that trains are being dispatched from an undisclosed location but none arrives and crowds of disgruntled passengers proliferate like bacteria in a petri dish.

◆

Was it a promotion of a demotion? I am transferred from a lively, high-traffic area of the office where I work to the quiet isolation of a small cubicle. I relinquish a solid oak portmanteau; I gain silence and privacy. It's a wash.

◆

A coyote slinks toward me, jumps on my

shoulders and begins to suck blood from the pores of my neck. I feel no pain and no resentment toward the beautiful canine.

"Drink, my pet," I say. "Drink your fill."

♦

I'm looking for the men's room in an ornate multistory building. I climb a number of stairs and reach a Chinese restaurant. A man sings in French. It's an Aznavour classic, *Sa Jeunesse*, an ode to fleeting youth. I exclaim, "What are the odds of hearing a song sung in French in a Chinese eatery … in California? I mean, I am in California, am I not?" The man continues to sing, this time *La Fleur Que tu M'avais Jetée*, an aria from Bizet's Carmen.

♦

Tiny insect-like white slimy creatures are coursing under the skin in my arms. My wife douses me with a mixture of ginger ale and Merlot, and the creatures crawl out and scurry in all directions.

In the next sequence, I catch a man rifling through my wife's pocketbook. I look for my gun but all I find is a toy pistol. The man surrenders but the police refuse to arrest him on the grounds that he is a pathetic human being who deserves pity, not prison. Such reasoning, I protest, is out of character for constabularies known to shoot first and ask questions later. Outraged, the cops arrest me instead and charge me with defamation of character. I am later tried, accused of sedition, and remanded to the Federal Dream Rehabilitation Penitentiary.

◆

In the first part of the dream, my wife and I are having an animated debate: California vs. New York. After better than sixteen years in the Golden State, accustomed to mild, sunny winters, recollections of whiteouts and ice storms and frozen toes sending shivers through my old bones, I favor the former. Neither is able to convince the other. After a very brief, gray, amorphous intermission, I find myself immersed in the second part of the dream. I'm at the beach somewhere in the South Pacific—Tahiti? I head for the surf but thousands of people frolic in the waves and there is no room for me to swim. I marvel at the height and power of the rolling surf but I resent the sea of humans bobbing around me.

I give a little girl my flippers, goggles and snorkel and dejectedly declare:

"I've had it. I'm going home."

♦

The garage door in the apartment building where I live is stuck halfway open. Armed with a key, I descend to the basement through a series of winding labyrinths and I manage to fix the door. No one seems to appreciate my good will.

Back in my apartment, someone rings the bell. I can hear a small dog panting. I open the door. It's my late mother. I let her in. We look at each other without saying a word.

♦

A small boy tells me that he composes music only he can hear. I urge him to hum a melody but he says he's unable to do so and that he's headed to Vienna where he hopes his music can be "extirpated" from his mind. I start singing the triumphant finale from Beethoven's Ninth Symphony. I am moved to tears when I discover that I am that boy.

♦

I check into a hotel and have to sign the credit card receipt but no matter how hard I try, I can't remember what my signature looks like. The pen disintegrates between my fingers.

♦

I dream I'm blind in one eye. I soon regain normal vision. I don't question the phenomenon. Looking at the bright side, I tell myself it wasn't blindness. Maybe I'd caught sight of a pretty damsel and winked at her.

♦

Was it Reena? I'm not sure. Maybe it was Rose or Regina or Rebecca or Ruth. It's hard to remember all the identities they assume on my nightly outings. I pick them up at the House of Limbo where young native girls give themselves to a dreamer for a meal, a hot shower, a clean bed and the short-lived illusion that raw, crapulous sex can somehow lead to love. I show them a good time. I treat them with kindness; I find the experience ennobling. Kindness has a way of humanizing exploitation. I never pay for my pleasure. I buy them groceries instead. Theirs is a risky occupation and there are always five or six other mouths to feed in the slums of Britton Hill. The slums are filled with precious dreams but I know they will never get past the shacks that overlook the sea.

◆

Doing laps in the pool, I see black and purple clouds rolling in from the northwest. A single lightning bolt rips the sky from zenith to horizon line. A piercing thunderclap follows. My arms and legs have turned to jelly and I struggle to hoist myself out of the water. Wet, trembling, I climb over a chain-link fence and roll down a mossy embankment.

◆

His eyes ablaze, pacing restlessly like a man possessed, his fingers clawing at invisible monsters, the preacher at the Apocalypse Now Baptist Church in Benton, Arkansas, is quoting from St. John the Divine [who plagiarized, without attribution, the same delusions that had haunted Ezekiel seven centuries earlier]:

> *"… And the first beast was like a lion, and the second beast like a calf, and the third beast had a face as a man, and the fourth beast was like a*

flying eagle. And the four beasts had each of them six wings about him...."

I walk up to the preacher and say, "If you repeat other people's demented fabrications, you're not just a clumsy liar, you're a dismal failure." Turning red, the pastor threatens me with the fires of hell. He then explodes like an overinflated balloon. Pieces of him float back to earth like volcanic ash. The sky darkens; I hear a loud, insistent jingle and the brisk sound of curtains being parted.

"Time to get up, honey," intones my wife. "You'll be late for work."

I groan. I retired sixteen years ago and no amount of coaxing can make me wake up, shave and shower, wolf down a hasty breakfast, put on a suit and tie, run for the train and toil for someone else, not even for a fetching salary, not even in a dream. My eyes part open briefly. I smile. It's Saturday. It was just a nightmare. I turn around, pull the comforter over my ears, spoon my wife and fall blissfully back to sleep.

ONE MORE FOR THE ROAD

Pity the dreamer. His travail is dissonant; his art off-key, his harvest seldom more than the disfigured remains of a vagabond spirit in search of his worldly self. To dream is to partake of a latent reality; or to break loose from reality inflicted. It is an act of emancipation from a vast realm where monsters, real and mythic, lie in wait. The journey is fraught with perils, the course is littered with ruses and hidden traps. You might not countenance what you discover along the way. The obvious is often unendurable. Some dreams are aimed to shock, not enchant, to scandalize, not amuse or pander to. Take the dream, suitably customized for the occasion, that a childhood memory reenacted the other night.

"For homework," says Monsieur Delorme, my 6th-grade teacher (who somehow hasn't aged), "write a composition. Tell me about your dreams."

I grumble. "Not again."

Monsieur Delorme insists. "It's been more than six decades since you entertained the class with your aerial escapades. This is another time and place. Surely you've landed safely and learned a thing or two. Come on, be a sport. One more dream for the road."

♦

It's summer 2015, somewhere in America. I'm pushing 78. A computer keyboard has long since replaced my old calligraphy nib and inkpot; a backlit screen—my lovingly tended notebooks. I let go with both barrels:

"Dawn. At first, they used their fangs, their claws. Later, they picked up a rock, a bough, a bone. They felt a great power surging through their fists, and the carnage began. At noon, bombs began to rain down. Fragmentation bombs rip, rend, slash, sever. Incendiary bombs

carbonize everything in sight. Concussion bombs produce shock waves that shatter granite. Napalm, like molten lead, sticks to flesh and devours it. Some bombs spread the plague. Others paralyze, asphyxiate, blind. Neutron bombs snuff out dreams but spare buildings and monuments and shrines. Binary projectiles pack twice the lethal punch of a single dose of nerve gas. In remote fiefdoms, mustard gas is king. There are bombs on the drawing board that are designed to kill the indigent, the sick, the feeble-minded, the mad, or the imprudently smart; bombs genetically programmed to annihilate certain races. There might even be a precision device that wipes out all septuagenarians, a bomblet expressly engineered to obliterate those who can't help but feel that more bombs are on the way, who say so out loud, and who know that there will soon be no good place left on Earth to hide, not even in a dream. For twilight is a-nearing."

♦

"So what's left," asks Monsieur Delorme. "So what's left," echo my former classmates. I look at them with a mixture of pity and impatience.

"Uncertainty. The thrill of impermanence.

*Randomness. Bedlam. Choose your own finale.
Rebels and despots will trade places and it will
be impossible to tell them apart. Earth will keep
producing would-be redeemers bent on saving
humanity – or else. The spider will spin her
web. The sun will rise. The cockerel will pro-
claim the birth of a new day, and we will spurt
out of our mothers' bellies, wet and cold, des-
tined to thrash about for a time on battlefields
and assembly lines, while the tax collector…."*

♦

My former classmates are all grown up now.
The would-be millionaire quadrupled his father's fortune. He cares not a whit about money, he says; he's in it for the wheeling and
dealing, the intrigues, the power plays, the
"game" as he calls it. Men like him fear failure
but they never anticipate the misery that their
success engenders. That's what makes them so
venal.

Marianne, the starry-eyed, pig-tailed ideal-
ist who dreamed of a world at peace is now a
graying, spindly grandmother whose dream
of peace has turned to dust.

Retired after fifty years of drudgery as a
lowly government paper-pusher, the once-
hopeful public servant joined the Front Na-

tional. He vents his frustration by blaming a lackluster career on foreigners, Arabs, blacks, Freemasons, gays and Jews. Especially Jews. That's the thanks you get for fabricating God, framing the Ten Commandments, and giving the world the Torah, Jesus, Karl Marx, Sigmund Freud, Albert Einstein and Woody Allen.

The aspiring battlefield commander never rose above the rank of sergeant. He lost an arm fighting in Algeria; his son died in Afghanistan, his grandson perished in the senseless tribal wars that convulse the Central African Republic. He speaks at rallies against the folly of war. He draws a great deal of applause but instigates no action. Meanwhile, the lords of capital and the cannon merchants salivate at the prospect of war. Pillaging the national treasury and fleecing taxpayers, they prosper when the first shot ring out. And so, military transports keep bringing home body bags and flag-draped caskets. Posthumous medals are cast to honor young people who die in unwinnable wars they did not choose to fight. Bugles play taps, and three rifle volleys ring out in the grief-filled stillness of a hundred village cemeteries.

The wannabe cowboy found another calling; he joined the priesthood and retired to a monastery nestling in a hidden valley at the foot of the Alps where contemplative monks have been praying for peace eighteen hours a day for the past one thousand years.

Instead of a toque blanche, a high-collared white double-breasted jacket, checkered pants and neckerchief, the future restaurateur settled for a café waiter's modest denim apron.

Not a single Pelé, Lionel Messi or Diego Maradona emerged from the budding foot-ballers of my childhood, only tired third-rate athletes who ran after a ball for a living and now can't walk without wincing. Marcel was no Muhammad Ali, Sugar Ray Robinson, Rocky Marciano or Joe Louis—only a punch-drunk drooling wretch who never earned a title fight.

They all look sad. Sadness is often the product of regret. It is the most haunting kind of sadness.

WHAT IF

It makes no sense to speak of "proper" or "improper" dreams, of "virtuous" or "sinful" ones. What dreamers conjure up is what is already there before them in the glaring light of day—but with a twist. It's the hyperbolic nature of dreams that transforms perceived reality into a grotesque parody of itself. But the essential truths dreams convey, even metaphorically, speak volumes about the dreamer.

If dreams are the portals to the soul, they are the gateway to the dreamer's deepest musings about the fullness and provisional nature of being. For me, to *be* raises interesting inferences. A part of me keeps wondering: Am I dreaming or am I being dreamed by someone dreaming he is me? The question, the province of ontology [the nature of existence] and epistemology [the nature of knowledge] is this: Where does dream end and reality begin? Are my ruminations spinoffs of direct experience or the undigested leftovers of wayward meditations? Is reality a dimension only an engaged observer can traverse and outlive? Or are dreamers casual and unwitting onlookers fated to replay reality through their mind's eye? These and other introspections not easily put into words and pondered time and time again in silent thought (and in my sleep) have yet to yield unambiguous answers. When words fail me, I paint brooding or surreal paintings. They now adorn the walls of my home and telegraph the deep inner unrest that inspired them. Most are so perplexing that I am often asked:

"What are you trying to say?"

I invariably respond, "I don't know. You tell me."

Having to explicate art is humiliating.

♦

Edgy, agitated, brimming with emotions that oscillate from rapture to exasperation, my dreams grapple with recondite memories and images of a future evocative of the inevitable finality of things. Dreams are no match for reality. Pitiless and cunning, reality always triumphs in the end. It is in solipsism that dreamers, philosophers, poets and mystics, musicians and artists and writers find inspiration. It is in dreams that the castaways seek comfort or meaning or shelter.

What I will need to ponder to the end of my days is this: Have I been dreaming the life I live? Am I the misshapen relic of someone else's fancy? Are fading memories of my beloved Paris, of my father's arrest by the French Gestapo, of my grandparents' murder at Auschwitz, of Bucharest and days spent cowering in subterranean shelters as U.S. heavy bombers conducted deadly strafing raids, of the Jerusalem of gold and copper and light where I experienced my fist orgasm (and nearly fainted), of my mother's brave but hopeless battle with pancreatic cancer, of a twenty-two-year failed first marriage to a woman who punished me for the duration because I wasn't the model husband she'd envisioned, of my older son's ignoble conversion to Messianic

Christianity, of his younger sibling's spiraling descent into melancholy and surliness, of New York and California and Barbados and Grenada and Costa Rica and Guatemala and Honduras and Molokai and Moscow nights spent waiting for daybreak: Are they all mere mental constructs lacking tangible being—like "God"?

◆

In a dream long ago that stretched the limits of credulity, I once spoke to "God." I said, "I have in me the need to find you but you've made yourself awfully scarce since my people fabricated you." God manifested the fullness of his impenetrability by staying hidden and speechless. All I heard was the echo of my own voice:

"Have I been weaving out of pure invisible cloth a reality that has no substance? Is surrendering to nothingness the essence of faith?" A distant voice retorted:

"Nothingness is the medium through which all energy moves, from above to below and from below to above. Below, in Man, is a sense of nothingness that transcends ego; above is a nothingness that transcends all boundaries and planes. The nothingness below fuses with the nothingness above, locking heaven and earth in eternal embrace. That is why God is found only amongst the truly humble."

Quantum physics couched in mysticism? Patronizing doubletalk? I am speechless.

♦

Sometimes dreams break free from their ethereal cocoons; they acquire tangible form. Who knows, perhaps you're all the illegitimate offspring of an overly fertile imagination. Can you say for sure that you exist outside my dreams? What if the notion that you're real, in any sense of the word, is a hallucination of my own confection? What if every fork in the road leads to another fork, every dream to another dream, every you to another you who owes his existence to another me?"

A TAWDRY CLICHÉ

As dawn alights and fog turns to manifest reality, I take stock of the dreams. I can't explain why so many of my escapades lead me through hotels and train stations. Nor do I understand why I keep meandering in maze-like streets, crawling through deformed, architecturally implausible edifices or getting stuck in forbidding dead-ends. But I know this: Hotels are the most hostile of all venues; they reek of impermanence and loneliness and anonymity and, even at their most elegant, of staleness and debauchery. So do the countless railroad depots in which I so often transit in the company of expressionless commuters. I also know that escape and entrapment, false leads and missed opportunities, strange encounters and waning memory, trains that never leave and trains that never reach their destination, elevators that have a will of their own, cryptic conversations, stolen pleasures and simmering hostility are *not* the disfigured remains of yesterday's musings and subconscious meditations. Instead, I think, they betray the fruitless exertions we make to find our "place" in the sun. To "get lost," literally or emblematically, as we all sometimes do in the course of a lifetime, to be trapped in eerie scenarios and discover ourselves back where we started, suggests that we all seek a pathway to a brighter reality. It is anticipation in its purest form. It is hope distilled. It is also an affirmation that when all is said and done, at the very conclusion of bizarre and aimless peregrinations, worn out and confused, we must bravely accept that some dreams are too close for comfort, while others are just not meant to be.

In the larger scheme of things, life is a wakeful dream. Reality is the lethal version of the dreams that lampoon it. In between is where intellect and fantasy, creativity and trickery intersect. One thing is clear: When we cease to dream, all that we *are* ceases to be.

So I dream on. Everything else is a tawdry cliché.

W. E. Gutman is a retired journalist. A former editor and writer at the late-great New York City-based futurist monthly, *OMNI*, he reported from Central America from 1994 to 2006. He has contributed hundreds of newspaper and magazine articles and is the author of nine books. He lives with his wife in southern California's "high desert."

www.ingramcontent.com/pod-product-compliance
Lightning Source LLC
Chambersburg PA
CBHW052207090426
42741CB00010B/2450